SAXON MATH™

Grades K–8

Scope and Sequence

- Math K–4

- Intermediate 3–5

- Courses 1–3

SAXON™

A Harcourt Achieve Imprint

www.SaxonPublishers.com
1-800-284-7019

SAXON MATH™
K-8 SCOPE AND SEQUENCE — TABLE OF CONTENTS

Saxon Math K–4... 1

Numbers and Operations..3

Measurement 12

Geometry..15

Patterns, Algebra, and Functions......................................16

Statistics, Data Analysis, and Probability 17

Problem Solving 19

Communication 20

Mathematical Reasoning..20

Connections 20

Saxon Math Intermediate 3–5.. 21

Numbers and Operations..23

Algebra..26

Geometry..26

Measurement 27

Data Analysis and Probability...28

Problem Solving 29

Communication 29

Mathematical Reasoning..29

Connections 30

Saxon Math Courses 1–3 (Grades 6–8)........................... 31

Numbers and Operations..33

Algebra..35

Geometry..36

Measurement 38

Data Analysis and Probability...39

Problem Solving 40

Communication 40

Mathematical Reasoning..41

Connections 41

Sᴀxᴏɴ **MATH** K-4

Scope and Sequence

The Scope and Sequence for the *Saxon K–4* mathematics series is intended to help educators view the progression of mathematical topics throughout the series. Topics are grouped into nine strands:

1. Numbers and Operations
2. Measurement
3. Geometry
4. Patterns, Algebra, and Functions
5. Statistics, Data Analysis, and Probability
6. Problem Solving
7. Communication
8. Mathematical Reasoning
9. Connections

The locators in the Scope and Sequence identify lessons in which direct instruction of a topic is presented. The first lesson where the concept is taught is referenced, and subsequent lessons are referenced only when the concept is extended. Occasional references to spans of The Meetings are included to show the daily practice of expanding skills and concepts.

SAXON MATH™
SCOPE AND SEQUENCE

The locators in this Scope and Sequence indicate where direct instruction on each topic can be found. Locators refer to lessons and Meetings (M). In *Saxon Math K*, every tenth lesson has two parts, and in *Saxon Math 1, 2, 3,* and *4* every fifth lesson has two parts; locators for these lessons are labeled -1 or -2.

	Saxon Math K	Saxon Math 1	Saxon Math 2	Saxon Math 3	Saxon Math 4
Numbers and Operations					
Number Sense and Numeration					
Counts by 1's	M1; 7, 41, 61	2, 20-1, 34, 99, 131	1, 76, 77	23	22
Counts backward	109	4, 34, 43, 56	M5	M1–120-2	
Counts by 2's	125; M22	47, 51, 56, 64	M14	29, 51	26
Counts by 5's	91, 92; M18	70-1, 98	32, 46, 49, 78	13, 23, 30-2, 39	22
Counts by 10's	64, 65, 67, 68; M11	43, 46, 85-1, 90-1, 131	28, 76, 77, 95-2	13, 23, 64	22, 33
Counts by 100's		93, 131, 132	76, 77, 95-2	M3–9, 17–21	97
Counts by 25's			93	36	12
Counts by 3's			M78	M41–54	30-1
Counts by 4's			M106	M51–66	26
Counts by 6's				M81–91	26
Counts by 7's				M24–41	30-1
Counts by 8's				M91–103	26
Counts by 9's				M76–85-2	30-1
Counts by 12's				M31–40-2	22
Counts by 1,000's				130-2	97
Counts by ½'s				54	14
Counts by ¼'s				M86–94	69
Counts by 11's					30-1
Matches sets and numbers	24, 42, 62, 73	2, 5, 9, 10-1, 19			
Counts and groups numbers in tens and ones	M4A; 13, 64, 65, 67, 68	46, 84, 93, 131, 133	37, 76, 113, 95-2	22, 52, 64, 67, 76	11, 13, 16, 41
Uses expanded form to represent numbers	67, 81, 113	M3–135	84	41, 104, 112	53
Writes digits 0–9	12	3, 5, 8			
Writes numbers using words		63		68, 78, 103, 106	32, 52
Reads and writes whole numbers to 30	21, 74, 111, 120-1, 130-1	3, 5, 8, 11–33	1, 4	3, 8	1
Reads and writes whole numbers to 100 (2-digit numbers above 30)		34–111	1, 4	3, 8	6
Reads and writes whole numbers to 1,000 (3-digit numbers)		112–135	74, 76	27, 34, 41, 64	25-1

	Saxon Math K	Saxon Math 1	Saxon Math 2	Saxon Math 3	Saxon Math 4
Numbers and Operations, continued					
Number Sense and Numeration, continued					
Reads and writes whole numbers to 10,000 (4-digit numbers)				64, 104	51, 52
Reads and writes whole numbers to 100,000 (5-digit numbers)				103, 130-2	51, 52
Reads and writes whole numbers to 1,000,000 (6-digit numbers)				103, 130-2	51, 52
Reads and writes whole numbers to 1,000,000,000 (9-digit numbers)					51, 52
Identifies numbers before, after, and between	48, 75	17, 52, 92			
Identifies numbers on a hundred number chart	M3, 4A	16, 34, 43, 52	1, 2, 13, 36	3, 9, 14	
Compares 1- and/or 2-digit whole numbers	71, 99, 102	9, 40-1, 92, 108	8, 81	8, 13	25-1
Orders 1- and/or 2-digit whole numbers	21, 35, 74	4, 9, 17, 20-1, 32, 92	49, 94	8, 13	25-1, 33
Compares 3-digit or larger whole numbers			81	34, 130-2	25-1, 33
Orders 3-digit or larger whole numbers			74, 77	34, 130-2	25-1, 33
Rounds numbers to the nearest ten		115-2	94, 98	18, 19, 31, 52, 62	13, 33, 119
Rounds numbers to the nearest hundred or thousand				72, 130-2	33, 119
Identifies place value for each digit in numbers to 100		85-1, 131, 133	38, 42, 76, 84	3	25-1, 33
Identifies place value for each digit in numbers to 1,000		131, 133	76, 84, 109	27, 41, 64, 76	51, 53
Identifies place value for each digit in numbers to 1,000,000				134	59
Identifies place value for each digit in numbers to 100,000,000				134	95-1
Represents 2-digit whole numbers using concrete materials and/or pictures	80-1, 132	51, 85-1, 131, 133	53, 74	15-1, 22, 37, 63, 116	70-1
Represents 3-digit or larger whole numbers using concrete materials and/or pictures		131, 133	76, 77	64	66
Identifies and describes equivalent sets	117, 118	4, 9, 82	128		
Estimates and counts collections of objects	64; M17	55-2, 84, 85-1, 131	95-2	130-2, 135	90-1, 128
Represents equivalent forms of the same number	65, 92, 113	21, 94, 101	34, 41, 42	22, 76, 94, 119, 131	5, 22, 26, 30-1, 36, 53, 97
Compares sets of objects and identifies sets with more, fewer, and the same	17, 71	9, 38, 76, 82, 108	8, 77, 81	30-2, 40-2, 55-2, A	12, 51

Numbers and Operations, *continued*

Number Sense and Numeration, *continued*

	Saxon Math K	Saxon Math 1	Saxon Math 2	Saxon Math 3	Saxon Math 4
Identifies sets with the greatest and least number of objects	58, 98	7, 9, 38	49, 74, 81	30-2, 40-2, 55-2, A	
Renames numbers using regrouping		85-2, 86	61, 63, 68, 73	22, 52, 67, 76	11, 16
Identifies multiples of a number			103, 130-1, 130-2	M71–121	3, 6, 22, 26, 29, 30-1, 97
Identifies factors of a number			115-1, 120-1, 125-1	120-2	26, 61, 94, 107, 109
Identifies prime and composite numbers				120-2	94, 96
Identifies the least common multiple of two numbers				M121–135	29
Identifies the greatest common factor of two numbers					107, 109
Squares numbers				63, 81	116, 122
Identifies perfect squares				63	116
Identifies and simplifies expressions with exponents				63	116, 117, 128
Finds square roots of perfect squares				81, D	116
Identifies and approximates square roots					122
Identifies cube roots and perfect cubes					128
Identifies rational numbers from pictures and draws pictures to show rational numbers	17, 24, 50-2	18, 55-1, 87, 107, 122	19, 23, 24, 34, 41, 83	11, 37, 40-1, 56, 130-2	17, 68, 79, 91
Locates rational numbers on a number line	109	77	25-1, 56, 94	51, 54, 55-2, 99, 123	27, 33, 88, 93, 99
Identifies even and odd numbers	125	51, 56, 58, 64, 68	13, 96, 97, 128	9	26
Identifies ordinal position	28, 37, 46, 59	11, 22, 65-2	7, 14, 16, 20-1	77	2
Identifies and creates pairs		64	37, 108	9	
Identifies dozen and half dozen		103	67	26	
Reads and writes Roman numerals				75-2	98
Identifies the approximate value of π					132

Concepts of Whole Number Operations

	Saxon Math K	Saxon Math 1	Saxon Math 2	Saxon Math 3	Saxon Math 4
Shows the meaning of addition	18, 27, 50-2, 89, 119	12, 15-1, 19, 21, 25-1, 36, 94, 114	5, 10-1, 29, 44	5, 11, 15-1, 52, 53, 126	5
Acts out to show addition situations	18, 27, 50-2, 89, 119	12, 15-1, 19, 25-1	8, 10-1	11	45-1

Numbers and Operations, continued

Concepts of Whole Number Operations, continued

	Saxon Math K	Saxon Math 1	Saxon Math 2	Saxon Math 3	Saxon Math 4
Uses manipulatives to model and solve addition problems	18, 27, 50-2, 89, 119	23, 32, 58, 76, 94	20-1, 61, 104, A	15-1, 73, 74, 93	45-1
Draws pictures to model and solve addition problems	50-2, 121, 122, 126	15-1, 21, 25-1	22	11	45-1
Creates addition problem situations	27, 73, 89, 119	15-1, 25-1	8, 22	11, 35-2, 66	45-1
Writes number sentences to show addition	117	21, 25-1	22	11, 35-2, 66	45-1
Identifies addends and sums		21, 40-1, 94	10-1	5, 15-1, 20-1	5
Identifies and uses the commutative and associative properties of addition		94, 114	10-1, 58	5	5
Shows the meaning of subtraction	18, 27, 80-2, 89, 127	12, 15-1, 33, 34, 44, 101	11, 22, 29, 60-1	10-1, 11, 20-1, 35-2, 91, 92, 126	23
Acts out to show subtraction situations	18, 27, 80-2, 89, 127	12, 15-1, 33, 101	11	11	59
Uses manipulatives to model and solve subtraction problems	18, 27, 80-2, 89, 127	49, 68, 101, 121, 132	87, 88, 127	73, 74, 91, 93	45-1
Draws pictures to model and solve subtraction problems	100-2, 128, 130-2	15-1, 33	22	11, 67	59
Creates subtraction problem situations	27, 89, 127	15-1, 33	11, 22	35-2	45-1
Writes number sentences to show subtraction		33, 101	22, 89, 91	11, 35-2	45-1
Identifies differences		125-1	75-1, 119	10-1, 60-1, 65-1, 75-1	11, 21
Uses the inverse relationship between subtraction and addition to check answers		101, 121, 125-1	29, 75-1, 80-1, 91	10-1, 20-1, 67, 92	62, 66
Writes addition and subtraction fact families		132, 134	29; M50-1, 53	15-1, 20-1, 25-1, 30-1, 35-1, 40-1	
Shows the meaning of multiplication		46, 93	92, 110-1, 116, 121, 130-2	45-1, 56, 57, 87, 116, 126	22
Acts out to show multiplication situations		46, 93	116	56	23, 31, 45-1, 60-1
Uses manipulatives to model and solve multiplication problems		46, 93	116	70-1, 87, 88	60-1, 61
Draws pictures to model and solve multiplication problems		79	110-1, 116	56, 57	23
Writes number sentences to show multiplication			92, 110-1, 117	56, 57	23
Identifies factors and products			115-1, 120-1, 125-1	45-1, 120-2	26

	Saxon Math K	Saxon Math 1	Saxon Math 2	Saxon Math 3	Saxon Math 4
Numbers and Operations, *continued*					
Concepts of Whole Number Operations, *continued*					
Makes, labels, and writes number sentences for an array			121, 122	87, 88	60-1, 61
Identifies and uses the commutative and associative properties of multiplication			115-1	85-1, 118, 120-1	26, 94, 97
Shows the meaning of division	70-1, 97, 102, 115, 125	109	96, 97, 120-1, 128	37, 107, 108	70-1, 83
Acts out to show division situations	70-1, 97, 102, 115, 125	109	128, 133	107	70-1
Uses manipulatives to model and solve division problems	70-1, 97, 102, 115, 125	109	120-1, 125-1	37, 107	70-1
Draws pictures to model and solve division problems			96, 97	37, 107	70-1
Writes number sentences to show division			128	107, 108	62, 76
Identifies the properties of 0 or 1 in multiplication and/or division			130-1	45-1, 59, 85-1	26
Uses the inverse relationship between division and multiplication to check answers			128	59, 105-1, 122	62, 76, 77, 83, 87, 101
Writes multiplication and division fact families				105-1	
Identifies quotients, dividends, and/or divisors				59	76
Uses a calculator to explore mathematical operations		B	A	D	90-1, 120-1, 122, 130-1, 132
Whole Number Computation					
Addition					
Uses concrete objects or pictures to model and solve addition problems	18, 27, 50-2, 89, 119	23, 32, 58, 76, 94	28, 61, 115-1	15-1, 73, 74, 76, 93	45-1
Identifies one more than a number	109	32, 34, 36, 37	2, 10-1		
Identifies ten more than a number		89, 90-1, 91	20-1, 36, 44	14, 31	
Masters addition facts to 18		27, 36, 41, 76, 94, 105-1	5, 10-1, 35-1, 55-1	5, 20-1, 25-1, 30-1, 35-1, 40-1	20-2, 25-2, 30-2, 35-2, 40-2
Identifies missing addends		94	35-1	5, 66, 101	55-1, 63
Estimates a sum		111, 115-1	98, 109	31, 52, 53, 73	13, 33, 41
Adds using mental computation		M41, 45-2, 66–70-1	20-1, 36, 44, 98	14, 31, 33, 42, 69	6, 11, 16

	Saxon Math K	Saxon Math 1	Saxon Math 2	Saxon Math 3	Saxon Math 4

Whole Number Computation, *continued*

Addition, continued

	Saxon Math K	Saxon Math 1	Saxon Math 2	Saxon Math 3	Saxon Math 4
Adds three or more single-digit numbers		114	58	38, 133	8
Adds 2-digit numbers without regrouping		73–75-1, 81, 91	44, 53, 54, 73	31, 33	11, 13
Adds two 2- or 3-digit numbers		73–75-1, 81, 86, 91	36, 53, 54, 61–64, 68, 73, 79, 109	52, 53, 69, 76	11, 13, 16, 33
Adds 3-digit numbers and money amounts (decimals)			109	82, 89, 106	13, 41, 42, 95-1
Adds three or more multidigit numbers			68	89	16
Adds two 4-digit or larger numbers				106	41
Adds whole numbers and money amounts (decimals) to $99,999.99				82, 89, 106	6, 8, 12, 13, 41, 95-1
Uses addition to check subtraction problems		101, 121, 125-1	29, 91	10-1, 20-1, 67, 92	66
Uses estimation to check the reasonableness of calculated results			109, B	52, 53	13, 33, 41
Identifies a missing digit in an addition problem			35-1, 40-1, 45-1, 50-1, 55-1	44	9, 55-1, 63
Solves problems involving addition	18, 50-2, 89, 119, 121	12, 15-1, 25-1	8, 22	11, 35-2, 49, 50-1, 52, 53, 90-1	45-1, 55-1, 59, 63
Writes story problems for addition number sentences				11, 35-2, 93, 126	45-1

Subtraction

	Saxon Math K	Saxon Math 1	Saxon Math 2	Saxon Math 3	Saxon Math 4
Uses concrete objects or pictures to model and solve subtraction problems	18, 27, 80-2, 89, 127	49, 68, 101, 121, 132	85-1, 87	73, 74, 91, 93	45-1
Identifies one less than a number	109	44, 45-1	2, 65-1		
Identifies ten less than a number		123	71	14, 62	
Masters subtraction facts with minuends to 10		68, 101, 102, 121, 132	29, 60-1, 65-1, 70-1, 75-1, 80-1, 85-1, 90-1, 95-1, 100-1, 105-1	10-1, 50-1	50-2, 55-2, 60-2, 65-2, 130-1
Masters subtraction facts with minuends of 11 to 18		A	60-1, 65-1, 70-1, 75-1, 80-1, 85-1, 90-1, 95-1, 100-1, 105-1	60-1, 65-1, 75-1, 80-1	50-2, 55-2, 60-2, 65-2, 130-1
Checks subtraction answers using addition		101, 121, 125-1	29, 91	10-1, 20-1, 67, 92	66
Estimates a difference			119	62, 72	58

Numbers and Operations, continued

Whole Number Computation, continued

Subtraction, continued

	Saxon Math K	Saxon Math 1	Saxon Math 2	Saxon Math 3	Saxon Math 4
Subtracts using mental computation			71	14, 62, 69	58
Subtracts 2-digit numbers without regrouping		127	71	14, 62	
Subtracts 2- or 3-digit numbers			87–89, 91, 119	67, 69, 72, 91, 92	66
Subtracts 3-digit numbers and money amounts (decimals)			119	92	66
Subtracts 4-digit or larger numbers					66
Solves problems involving subtraction	18, 27, 89, 127, 128	12, 15-1, 33	11, 22, 89	11, 35-2, 67, 86, 93, 96, 120-1	45-1, 55-1, 59, 63
Writes story problems for subtraction number sentences				35-2, 67, 75-1	45-1

Multiplication

	Saxon Math K	Saxon Math 1	Saxon Math 2	Saxon Math 3	Saxon Math 4
Doubles a number			132	70-1	125-1
Masters multiplying by 0, 1, 2, 3, 4, and 5			103, 110-1, 115-1, 120-1, 125-1, 130-1	45-1, 70-1, 85-1, 95-1, 100-1	55-1, 60-1, 65-1, 105-2, 110-2
Masters multiplying by 6, 7, 8, and 9				55-1, 110-1, 115-1, 120-1	55-1, 60-1, 65-1, 105-2, 110-2
Multiplies by 10, 100, 1,000, and/or 10,000			36, 103	45-1, 103	36
Multiplies by multiples of 10, 100, 1,000, and/or 10,000			92, 103	109, 122	97
Multiplies using mental computation			92, 103, 110-1, 115-1, 120-1, 125-1, 130-1	112	36, 38, 49, 73, 97
Multiplies a 2-digit number by a 1-digit number			103, A	116	38, 49, 73
Multiplies a 3-digit or larger number by a 1-digit number			103	116	54
Multiplies a 2-digit or larger number by a 2-digit number					73, 80-1
Makes and uses a multiplication table			130-2	120-1	43
Uses multiplication to check division problems				105-1, 124, 132	62, 76, 77, 83, 87, 101
Multiplies using the multiplication algorithm				116	49, 54, 73, 80-1
Solves problems involving multiplication			92, 103, 110-1, 116, 117	40-1, 56, 57, 63, 88, 125-1, 135	73, 80-1, 123

	Saxon Math K	Saxon Math 1	Saxon Math 2	Saxon Math 3	Saxon Math 4

Whole Number Computation, *continued*

Division

	Saxon Math K	Saxon Math 1	Saxon Math 2	Saxon Math 3	Saxon Math 4
Divides sets of objects into equal groups	97, 102, 125	109	120-1, 125-1, 133	9, 56, 57	
Divides by 2	70-1, 125, 134	18, 67	128	37	62
Masters division facts				59, 90-1	105-1, 110-1, 115-2, 120-2, 135
Writes division problems in three ways				59, 90-1, 105-1	62, 76
Divides using mental computation				122	104
Divides 2- and/or 3-digit multiples of 10 by a 1-digit number				122	87, 101
Divides a 2-, 3-, and/or 4-digit number by a 1-digit number				122, 124, 132	76, 77, 83, 84, 87, 90-1, 101, 123
Checks division answers using multipication				105-1, 124, 132	62, 76, 77, 83, 87, 101
Divides using the division algorithm				132	77, 87, 101
Solves problems involving division	70-1, 97, 115, 132, 134	109	128, 133	37, 107, 108, 124, 125-1	70-1, 76, 83, 123

Fractions and Decimals

	Saxon Math K	Saxon Math 1	Saxon Math 2	Saxon Math 3	Saxon Math 4
Identifies one half and/or one fourth of a whole	70-1, 115, 132, 134	18, 55-1, 67, 88	19, 23, 24, 34, 39, 41	17, 24, 25-2	17, 40-1
Identifies a fractional part of a whole	70-1, 115, 132, 134	18, 55-1, 67, 88, 107, 117	19, 23, 24, 39	17, 21, 24, 25-2, 93, 94	17, 40-1
Writes a fraction to show a part of a whole		55-1	59, 83	24, 25-2, 74, 93, 94	17, 40-1
Represents and writes mixed numbers			111, 112	98, 99, 119	78, 79, 84
Finds half of a set of objects	97	109	83, 96, 97	37, 111	106
Indentifies a fractional part of a set		122	59, 83, 96, 97, 128	26, 61, 111	106
Writes a fraction to show a part of a set			59, 83	26, 61	106
Compares fractions	134	67, 107	34, 41	73, 74, 93, 94	27, 28, 68, 69, 88
Recognizes and identifies equivalent fractions			41	94	68, 96
Orders fractions				73, 74, 93, 94	27, 28, 68, 69, 88
Simplifies fractions					98, 109
Writes fraction number sentences that equal 1				25-2	

	Saxon Math K	Saxon Math 1	Saxon Math 2	Saxon Math 3	Saxon Math 4
Numbers and Operations, *continued*					
Fractions and Decimals, *continued*					
Adds and subtracts fractions				73, 74, 93, 94	91, 95-1, 102, 127
Uses pictures to represent decimal fractions				131	91, 95-1
Writes tenths or hundredths using common and decimal fractions				78, 119, 131	88, 95-1, 118
Identifies fraction, decimal, and/or percent equivalents				78, 119, 131	118
Finds the percent of a number					120-1
Adds money amounts (decimals)			53, 54, 61, 62, 109	82, 89, 106	6, 8, 12, 13, 41, 95-1
Subtracts money amounts (decimals)			87, 88, 119	96	66, 95-1
Multiplies and/or divides money amounts (decimals)				M127	38, 54, 77, 87, 101, 120-1, 123
Money					
Identifies and counts pennies	41, 42, 44, 51, 130-1	16, 51, 53, 85-1, 116	28, 51, 107	23, 36	12
Identifies and counts dimes	65, 67, 68, 113	46, 53, 66, 85-1, 116	28, 51, 107	13, 23, 36	12
Identifies and counts nickels	91, 92, 94, 96, 113	98, 99, 116, 126	46, 51, 107	13, 23, 36	12
Identifies and/or counts quarters	113, 116	126	93, 107	36	12
Identifies one-dollar bills	113	105-2, 113	127	36	
Finds the value of a set of coins	51, 67, 92, 113, 116	46, 66, 99, 116, 126	46	13, 23, 36	12
Trades pennies for dimes and nickels	65, 91	53, 85-2, 86, 98	42, 61–63, 87–89	22, 96	41
Compares the values of sets of coins			46	13	12
Finds the value of a set of coins and bills					63
Reads and writes money amounts to $1.00 using dollar and cent symbols	49, 51	16, 66, 105-2, 113	86, 109, 119	28, 36	13
Reads and writes money amounts to $10.00			86, 109, 119	28, 36	14, 123
Reads and writes money amounts to $99,999.99				78, 106	66
Selects coins for a given amount	116	66, 126	28	22, 79	12
Pays for items and/or makes change using coins	51, 68, 94, 116	66, 73–75-1, 86	127	22, 79	12
Makes change from $1.00, $5.00, and/or $10.00			127	102; M121–135	55-1, 63
Counts bills		105-2, 113		76, 91	63
Pays for items using bills		113	127	76, 91	63

Numbers and Operations, continued

	Saxon Math K	Saxon Math 1	Saxon Math 2	Saxon Math 3	Saxon Math 4
Money, continued					
Adds and subtracts money amounts (decimals)		73–75-1, 86, 127	53, 54, 61–64, 109, 119	82, 89, 96, 106	13, 41, 95-1, 66, 67
Writes checks				78, 106	32, 42
Balances a checkbook register					67
Completes a catalog order form					42
Determines unit cost				125-1	
Estimates and finds amount of sales tax				M127	130-1

Measurement

	Saxon Math K	Saxon Math 1	Saxon Math 2	Saxon Math 3	Saxon Math 4
Calendar and Time					
Identifies seasons	82, 135				2
Identifies today's date	M1–25	1	M1–135	M1–11	1
Identifies dates on a calendar	M1–25	M1–135	M1–135	1	1, 2, 24
Solves problems using a calendar	M19, 21, 23, 25	M18–135	M12	84	24; M1–135
Writes the date using digits			47; M48, 49	16	1
Identifies yesterday, today, and tomorrow	M19	M1–135	M1	M1–5	
Identifies days of the week and/or months of the year	M1–25	M1–135	16	M1–35	1, 24
Identifies weekdays and days of the weekend			16	M1–11	
Identifies morning, afternoon, evening, and night	124	11, 35-1	67	39	7
Identifies a.m., p.m., noon, and midnight			67	39	7
Uses digital and analog clocks to tell and show time	45, 47	48, 57, 87	3, 12, 26, 78, 106, 123	1, 4, 39, 71, 97	7
Tells and shows time to the hour	45, 47	48, 57	3, 12; M4–26	1	7
Tells and shows time to the half hour		87	26	4	7
Tells and shows time to the quarter hour			123	97	34
Tells and shows time to the 5-minute interval and/or minute			78	39, 71	7
Tells and shows time to the second					7, 34
Estimates time to the nearest half hour				4	
Identifies days of the week when regularly scheduled events occur	40-1				
Sequences daily events	30-1, 124	11, 35-1			
Compares events according to duration	65, 91, 113	100-1			

	Saxon Math K	Saxon Math 1	Saxon Math 2	Saxon Math 3	Saxon Math 4
Measurement, *continued*					
Calendar and Time, *continued*					
Orders events by time		11, 35-1, 100-1			
Identifies activities that take one hour, one minute, and one second			106		
Identifies equivalent units of time			106	39, 84	7, 22, 24, 36
Finds elapsed time			12	1, 4, 65-2	44
Identifies United States time zones					37
Temperature					
Identifies cold, cool, warm, and/or hot	100-1	128, C	M1–14		
Compares differences in hourly, daily, and/or seasonal temperature	82, 124, 135	128; M2–135	M1–135	70-2	
Compares situations and objects by relative temperature	100-1	C		46	
Reads a Fahrenheit thermometer		128, C	27, 69	18, 29, 46	74, 75-1
Estimates temperature			27	46, 84	74
Identifies common temperatures			69	18, 29, 46	74
Reads a Celsius thermometer				83	74, 75-1
Linear Measure					
Compares the length or height of objects	83, 120-2, 131	4, 7, 62, 104	8, 55-2, 99, 102	85-2	18, 19, 43, 88, 126
Orders objects by length or height	84, 87, 93	9, 62	99		
Creates a measuring tool	126	104			
Estimates and measures length or distance using nonstandard units	87, 106, 126	35-2, 62, 95-2	40-2	85-2	
Estimates length or distance	106	35-2, 95-2, 104	55-2	6, 32, 85-2	39, 88, 103
Selects and/or uses appropriate tools for measuring length	133	71, 97, 104, 119	102	6, 54, 85-2	39
Measures length using customary units (inch, foot, and yard)	133	97, 104	40-2, 43, 55-2, 72, 99, 102, 104	6, 85-2	14, 15-1, 18, 28, 39, 69, 103, 126
Draws line segments using customary units (inch)		97	56, 72	6	15-1, 19, 28, 69, 126
Measures length using metric units (centimeter, millimeter, and meter)		119	102, 104	32, 85-2, 114	14, 15-1, 39, 88
Draws line segments using metric units (centimeter and millimeter)		119	102	32, 43, 114, 119	15-1
Compares the size of the unit and the number of units used to measure an object		95-2	40-2		56
Identifies equivalent units of linear measure				85-2, 114	14, 22, 28, 29
Uses a scale to find distance on a map				125-2, 127	43

	Saxon Math K	Saxon Math 1	Saxon Math 2	Saxon Math 3	Saxon Math 4
Measurement, continued					
Weight (Mass)					
Compares and orders objects by weight (mass)	53, 72	29, 39	35-2, 110-2, 131	95-2	72
Weighs objects using nonstandard units	72	39, 135	35-2, 40-2		
Estimates weight (mass)	72, 106	29, 39, 135	35-2, 131	95-2	72
Selects and/or uses appropriate tools for measuring weight	53, 72	135	131	95-2	72
Identifies customary and/or metric units of mass		135	110-2, 131	95-2	72
Weighs objects using customary or metric units			110-2, 131	95-2	72
Capacity (Volume)					
Compares and/or orders containers by capacity	90-1, 120-1	50-1	75-2	45-2, 60-2	92
Identifies customary and/or metric units of capacity (cup, quart, gallon, and liter)	78	50-1, 110-1	45-2, 50-2, 75-2	45-2, 60-2, 65-2	92, 125-1
Selects and/or uses appropriate tools for measuring capacity	77, 78	50-1, 55-2, 110-1	50-2	45-2, 60-2	92, 125-1
Estimates capacity	78, 90-1, 120-1	50-1, 55-2, 110-1	75-2	45-2, 55-2	92
Measures capacity	77, 78, 90-1, 120-1	50-1, 55-2, 110-1	45-2, 50-2, 75-2	45-2, 60-2	92
Identifies and uses measuring cups	77	50-1, 110-1	45-2, 50-2, 75-2	45-2, 60-2, 65-2	125-1
Identifies and uses measuring spoons (tablespoon, teaspoon, and ½ teaspoon)			45-2	60-2	125-1
Follows a recipe and measures ingredients	77		45-2, 50-2	60-2, 65-2	125-1
Identifies equivalent units of capacity			75-2	45-2, 60-2	92
Area, Perimeter, and Volume					
Compares and orders objects by size (area)	105, 112, 115	75-2	9	10-2, 15-2, 63	82
Finds area using nonstandard units		75-2	100-2, 115-2, 129	88	82
Estimates area		75-2	115-2	88	82
Finds area of a rectangle			115-2, 129	88	56, 57
Finds the length of a side of a square given the area				81	
Finds perimeter of a polygon			104	49, 50-2	103
Uses perimeter formulas			104	49, 50-2, 88	134
Compares, estimates, and measures circumference					132

	Saxon Math K	Saxon Math 1	Saxon Math 2	Saxon Math 3	Saxon Math 4
Measurement, *continued*					
Area, Perimeter, and Volume, *continued*					
Finds volume of a rectangular prism				121	129
Finds volume of a cube				121	128
Geometry					
Spatial Relationships and Geometric Shapes					
Identifies right and left	103	7	1, 2		
Identifies first, last, between, and middle	28, 37, 46, 48, 75	2, 3, 5, 8, 11	7, 16		
Describes, compares, and orders concrete objects by relative position and attributes	12, 23, 32, 43, 53, 72, 83, 84, 87, 93	7, 11, 14, 17, 52	6, 9, 21, 25-2, 30-2		
Gives and follows directions about location	12, 48, 75	7, 19, 38	1, 2, 7		
Arranges and describes objects in relative space	12	7, 19, 38	124		
Makes and covers designs with pattern blocks or tangrams	14, 15, 29, 79, 105, 108, 114	31, 42, 60-1, 65-1	7, 10-2, 15-2, 85-2, 90-2, 100-2	10-2, 15-2	71
Makes and copies designs on a geoboard	56, 57, 63, 86, 100-2	14, 83, 96	57, 60-2, 65-2, 70-2		65-1, 81, 85-1, 86
Creates, identifies, and/or draws congruent shapes, designs, and/or line segments	63, 86	45-2, 83, 96	60-2, 65-2, 108, 118	6, 12, 17, 32, 58	71
Creates and/or identifies similar shapes	105		60-2, 65-2		71
Combines geometric shapes to make new shapes		75-2	24, 70-2, 80-2	50-2	56
Identifies, describes, sorts, and/ or compares two-dimensional geometric shapes	19, 23, 31, 57	6, 13, 24, 26, 124	18, 60-2, 65-2	7, 10-2, 100-2, 115-2	64, 71, 81, 82, 85-1, 86
Identifies, describes, and classifies polygons	19, 23, 31, 54, 85, 105	6, 13, 24, 26, 124	6, 18, 21, 25-2, 30-2, 57	7, 10-2, 20-2, 50-2, 100-2	64, 71, 81, 82, 85-1, 86
Identifies angles and sides		6, 13, 14, 24	57, 114, 118, C	7, 20-2, 43, 100-2	81, 114
Identifies parallel lines and line segments			108, 118	48, 100-2, 105-2	65-1
Identifies intersecting and perpendicular lines and line segments			118	105-2, 129	65-1
Identifies horizontal, vertical, and oblique line segments			33, 43, 104	48, 105-2	15-1
Names line segments				43	14, 15-1, 28, 69, 126

	Saxon Math K	Saxon Math 1	Saxon Math 2	Saxon Math 3	Saxon Math 4

Geometry, *continued*

Spatial Relationships and Geometric Shapes, *continued*

	Saxon Math K	Saxon Math 1	Saxon Math 2	Saxon Math 3	Saxon Math 4
Identifies right angles			114, 118, C	7, 100-2, 113	65-1, 85-1, 108, 111, 121, 124
Identifies acute and obtuse angles			C	113	124, 131, 135
Identifies straight angles					108, 111
Identifies supplementary angles					135
Identifies right triangles			114	113	108, 124, 135
Names triangles by angle size (acute, obtuse, or right)			C	113	124, 131
Identifies and classifies triangles by lengths of sides (scalene, isosceles, and equilateral)				43	131
Constructs scalene, isosceles, and equilateral triangles				43	131
Identifies and sorts concrete objects by attribute	23, 32, 43, 54	6, 13, 24, 26	6, 9, 21, 25-2, 30-2		113
Identifies, describes, sorts, compares, and/or constructs three-dimensional geometric solids	93, 112, 123	112, 120-1, 125-2	101	15-2, 115-2	113
Identifies faces, vertices, and edges of a geometric solid				115-2	113, 114

Transformations and Symmetry

	Saxon Math K	Saxon Math 1	Saxon Math 2	Saxon Math 3	Saxon Math 4
Identifies and draws a line of symmetry and/or creates symmetrical designs	129	54, 55-1	52	58	46
Explores, identifies, and/or shows transformations: translations (slides), rotations (turns), and reflections (flips)	108, 114	D	124	110-2	47, 89

Patterns, Algebra, and Functions

Patterns and Sequences

	Saxon Math K	Saxon Math 1	Saxon Math 2	Saxon Math 3	Saxon Math 4
Identifies, reads, and extends patterns in shapes, colors, designs, and/or numbers	9, 25, 33, 52, 55, 66, 88, 101	26, 58, 59	7, 15-2, 20-2, 30-1	M1–135	20-2
Identifies the missing shape or design in a repeating pattern	M3–25	26	15-2, 20-2	M101–106	
Identifies the missing number in a sequence	21, 35, 38	52	M18	5	9
Identifies the missing item(s) in an array or matrix	23, 32, 54	52	36	M91–100-2	61
Makes, labels, and writes number sentences for an array			121, 122	87	60-1, 61

Readiness for Algebraic Reasoning

	Saxon Math K	Saxon Math 1	Saxon Math 2	Saxon Math 3	Saxon Math 4
Constructs a number line and/or locates points on a number line	48, 75, 109	77, 80-1, 92	56, 94	51, 54, 55-2, 123	27, 33, 88

	Saxon Math K	Saxon Math 1	Saxon Math 2	Saxon Math 3	Saxon Math 4
Patterns, Algebra, and Functions, continued					
Readiness for Algebraic Reasoning, continued					
Graphs large numbers on a number line				55-2	33
Shows addition, subtraction, and/or multiplication on a number line				126	93
Locates and graphs points (ordered pairs) on a coordinate graph			126	129, 130-1	110-1, 133
Graphs linear functions on a coordinate plane					133
Simplifies expressions containing addition, subtraction, multiplication, and division				118, 133	117
Uses the order of operations to simplify expressions				38, 118, 133	117
Simplifies expressions containing parentheses				38, 118, 133	117, 134
Simplifies expressions containing exponents				63	116, 117, 128
Adds positive and negative numbers				128	93, 99
Relations and Functions					
Writes and solves number sentences for problems involving addition or subtraction		21, 25-1, 33, 132, 134	22, 89	11, 35-2, 52, 53, 66, 93, 126	45-1
Creates problems for addition and subtraction number sentences		15-1, 25-1	22, 89	35-2	45-1
Writes and solves number sentences for problems involving multiplication or division			117, 128	56, 57, 107, 108	23, 70-1
Creates problems for multiplication and division number sentences					31
Uses comparison symbols (>, <, and =)		108	81	47, 130-2	21, 25-1, 122
Represents an unknown using a symbol		94	30-1, 35-1, 40-1, 45-1, 50-1, 55-1	5	9
Identifies and writes a function rule				117	105-1, 133
Uses a function rule to complete a table				117	105-1, 133
Graphs linear functions on a coordinate plane					133
Statistics, Data Analysis, and Probability					
Data and Statistics					
Identifies an object that doesn't belong to a group	50-1				
Sorts and classifies objects by common attributes	23, 32, 43, 54, 85	13, 15-2, 38, 60-1, 122	21, 25-2, 30-2, 46, 65-2, 85-2		

	Saxon Math K	Saxon Math 1	Saxon Math 2	Saxon Math 3	Saxon Math 4
Data and Statistics, continued					
Identifies a sorting rule	34, 60-2	13, 15-2, 38, 60-1, 122	21, 25-2, 30-2, 46, 85-2		71
Determines questions for a survey	122		125-2	40-2	3, 35-1
Conducts a survey and/or records data	122		125-2	40-2	3, 35-1
Tallies data		70-1, 72, 98	32, 113, 125-2	30-2, 40-2, 80-2	35-1, 100-1, 115-1
Collects and sorts data	122	10-1, 38, 60-1, 72, 118	2, 17, 31, 32, 39, 48, 66, 82, 105-2, 113, 120-2, 125-2, 134, 135	2, 30-2, 40-2, 70-2, 80-2	2, 3, 35-1, 90-1, 104
Finds the range and mode of a set of data	69, 73	38	135	A, E	20-1
Finds the median of a set of data			77	A	112
Finds the mean (average) of a set of data				B, E	90-1, 104, 112
Uses a calculator to compare data			A, B	E	90-1, 104, 120-1, 122, 130-1, 132
Graphing					
Makes a real graph	11, 17, 22, 58, 69	5, 38, 65-1			
Graphs a picture on a pictograph	5, 82, 107, 135	7, 9, 38, 82	17, 82, 105-2	40-2	2, 50-1
Graphs data on a bar graph	11, 22, 58, 90-2	5, 7, 10-1, 19, 38, 40-1, 65-1, 82, 118	2, 31, 39, 48, 134, 135	2, 40-2, 55-2, 70-2, 80-2, 105-2	3, 10-1
Identifies most, more, fewest, less, and/or same on a graph	11, 17, 22	7, 9, 38, 65-1, 82, 118	2, 31, 39, 48, 135	2, 40-2, 55-2	
Draws conclusions, answers questions, and writes observations about a graph		10-1, 19, 40-1, 65-1, 82, 118	2, 17, 31, 39, 48, 105-2, 125-2, 134, 135	2, 40-2, 55-2, 70-2, 80-2, 105-2	3, 10-1, 20-1
Draws and reads a pictograph			17, 82, 105-2	2, 40-2	2, 50-1
Draws and reads a bar graph			2, 31, 39, 48, 113	2, 55-2	3, 10-1, 104
Draws and reads a bar graph with a scale greater than 1			113	55-2	3, 10-1, 50-1, 104
Draws and reads a line graph			M70-1	70-2	104
Creates and reads a Venn diagram			48, 66	105-2	48
Makes and reads a line plot				A	20-1
Draws and reads a circle (pie) graph					40-1
Makes a stem-and-leaf plot					112

	Saxon Math K	Saxon Math 1	Saxon Math 2	Saxon Math 3	Saxon Math 4
Statistics, Data Analysis, and Probability, continued					
Probability					
Describes the likelihood of an event	124	130-1	120-2, 135	80-2, 90-2, C	100-1, 115-1
Conducts a probability experiment		130-1	120-2, 135	80-2, 90-2, C	100-1, 115-1
Predicts the outcome of a probability experiment		130-1	120-2, 135	80-2, 90-2, C	100-1, 115-1
Determines the fairness of a game				90-2	
Problem Solving					
Developing Skills for Problem Solving					
Identifies steps in a process	30-1, 40-1	10-2	10-1	10-1	1; M1
Classifies and categorizes information	19, 23, 31, 32, 34, 43, 50-1, 85, 105	13, 35-1, 112, 130-1	2, 17, 31, 32, 48, 82, 113, 120-2, 125-2, 134, 135	7, 12, 20-2, 100-2, 113, 115-2	2, 3, 35-1, 90-1, 104
Identifies important/unimportant information		33	M23	35-2	
Looks for a pattern	40-2, 110-2	M7; 30-2, 60-2	7, 15-2, 30-1, 60-1, 100-1	70-1, 80-1	9, 105-1
Makes predictions	124	11, 100-1, 130-1	120-2, 134	80-2, D	100-1, 115-1
Chooses appropriate methods for finding the answers to problems		10-2, 80-2	10-1, 70-1, 100-1, B	10-1, 70-1, 80-1, E	10-2
Strategies for Problem Solving					
Acts out a problem or makes a model	18, 50-2, 60-2, 80-2, 89, 119	12, 15-1, 80-2, 110-2, 120-2	8, 11, 40-1, 77, 116	11, 30-1, 56, 64, 107	70-1
Draws a picture	50-2, 80-2, 100-2, 110-2, 121, 128, 130-2	15-1, 25-1, 50-2, 90-2, 130-2	22, 23, 76, 96, 116	11, 40-1, 56, 57, 70-1, 80-1, 107	20-2, 23, 50-2, 70-1
Guesses, checks, and revises	70-2, 90-2, 120-2	80-2, 120-2	70-1	30-1, 60-1, 120-1	33, 70-2, 74, 130-2
Looks for a pattern	40-2, 110-2	M7; 30-2, 60-2	7, 15-2, 30-1, 60-1, 100-1	70-1, 80-1	9, 30-2, 50-2, 105-1
Uses logical reasoning		10-2, 40-2	10-1	10-1, 20-1	10-2, 80-2, 90-2, 100-2, 110-2
Writes a number sentence		25-1, 33, 101	22, 89, 91, 92	11, 35-2, 66, 93, 107, 108, 126	23, 45-1, 70-1
Makes an organized list		20-2, 100-2	40-1	10-1, 22, 34, 50-1, 100-1	4, 130-2
Makes a table or chart		130-2	2, 32, 48, 82, 113	40-1, 70-1, 80-1, 110-1, 130-1	3, 40-2, 43

	Saxon Math K	Saxon Math 1	Saxon Math 2	Saxon Math 3	Saxon Math 4
Problem Solving, *continued*					
Strategies for Problem Solving, *continued*					
Simplifies the problem			40-1, 80-1, 100-1	31, 52, 60-1, 80-1, 110-1, 130-1	11, 16, 38, 119, 130-1
Works backward to solve a problem				20-1, 90-1, 120-1	
Communication					
Questions and responds	1–135	1–135	1–135	1–135	1–135
Works with partners or in groups	21, 52, 73, 99, 118	4–109	6, 16	7–135	1–135
Communicates mathematical ideas through objects, words, pictures, numbers, technology, and symbols	M1–25	B; M1–135	M1–135	M1–135	M1–135
Writes about math		118	4, 22, 29, 47, 84, 86, 92, 105-2, 111, 128	10-1, 80-2	10-2
Mathematical Reasoning					
Recognizes patterns	23, 33, 66, 95	26, 30-2, 60-2	7, 15-2, 20-2, 30-1	M1–135	
Classifies and sorts	16, 19, 23, 31, 57, 105, 113	13, 24, 38, 60-1, 72, 122	6, 9, 18, 21, 25-2, 30-2, 60-2, 65-2, 101	7, 12, 20-2, 100-2, 115-2	64, 71, 81, 85-1, 113
Solves spatial problems	15, 63, 105	14, 31, 42, 60-1, 65-1	1, 2, 7, 124	10-2, 15-2, 50-2	71, 86
Estimates	64, 90-1, 106, 120-1	35-2, 50-1, 62, 111, 115-2	35-2, 55-2, 75-2, 95-2, 98, 115-2	4, 6, 32, 46, 52, 62, 72, 85-2, 95-2	33, 90-1, 103, 122, 129
Explains an answer	40-2, 50-2, 60-2, 70-2, 80-2, 90-2, 100-2	M4–135	10-1	10-1	10-2
Connections					
Connects math to everyday life	45, 47, 49, 51, 68, 81, 94, 96, 116, 124	55-2, 66, 72, 87, 118, 128	17, 18, 37, 83, 86	1, 4, 28, 39, 65-2, 78, 84, 102	24, 32, 41, 44, 130-1
Connects math to science	77, 122	38, 39, 50-1, 128, 130-1, C	2, 17, 31, 50-2, 120-2, 134, 135, B	29, 40-2, 46, 65-2, 130-1	72, 74, 75-1, 112, 125-1
Connects math to social studies	122		125-2	40-2, 125-2, 127	39, 43, 50-1

SAXON MATH™
Intermediate 3–5

Scope and Sequence

The Scope and Sequence for the *Saxon Intermediate 3–5* mathematics series is intended to help educators view the progression of mathematical topics throughout the series. Topics are grouped into nine strands:

1. Numbers and Operations
2. Measurement
3. Geometry
4. Patterns, Algebra, and Functions
5. Statistics, Data Analysis, and Probability
6. Problem Solving
7. Communication
8. Mathematical Reasoning
9. Connections

The locators in the Scope and Sequence identify lessons in which direct instruction of a topic is presented. Once a topic is presented, students are continually exposed to the topic in the daily problem sets that follow. Because of space considerations, the daily problem sets are not referenced in the Scope and Sequence. Consequently, student exposure to individual topics is actually stronger than indicated on the following pages.

SAXON MATH™
SCOPE AND SEQUENCE

The locators in this Scope and Sequence indicate where direct instruction on each topic can be found. Locators refer to lesson and investigation numbers.

	Intermediate 3	Intermediate 4	Intermediate 5
Numbers and Operations			
Numeration			
Uses digits to write numbers	11, 32	3, 5, 10	1, 4, 7
Reads and writes whole numbers through 999	12	7	
Reads and writes whole numbers through 999,999	32	33	7
Reads and writes whole numbers through 999,999,999		34	
Reads and writes whole numbers through 999,999,999,999			52
Identifies place value through hundreds	11	4	3
Identifies place value through hundred thousands	32	33	
Identifies place value through hundred millions		34	
Identifies place value through hundred billions			52
Locates and names whole numbers on a number line	4, 15, 17, 33	Investigation 1	12, 27, 33
Reads and writes numbers in expanded form	11, 13, 14	16, 33	3, 48
Reads and writes numbers in expanded notation			48, 52, 78
Uses comparison symbols (=, <, >)	17, 27	56, 91, 103	4
Compares and orders whole numbers	17, 27, 39, 99, 103	5, 7, 33, 34; Investigation 1	4, 7
Basic operations			
Addition			
Models addition	6, 9, 13, 16	1	6, 41
Adds whole numbers	6, 8, 9, 10, 13, 16, 18, 24, 36, 92, 94	1, 2, 11, 13, 45	6, 8, 10, 24
Adds decimal numbers	22, 25, 92, 94	8, 22, 43, 50, 91	13, 73, 99
Adds fractions and mixed numbers			41, 43, 116
Uses regrouping in addition	13, 16		6
Finds the value of a collection of coins and bills	21, 22, 25, 81; Investigation 2	8, 22	
Subtraction			
Models subtraction	7, 14, 19	34	9, 41, 43, 59, 63
Subtracts whole numbers	7, 8, 14, 19, 20, 23, 28, 40, 92, 94	6, 12, 14, 16, 25, 41	8, 9, 14, 16, 24
Subtracts decimal numbers	26, 92, 94	30, 43, 50, 91	13, 73, 99, 102
Subtracts fractions and mixed numbers			41, 43, 59, 63, 116
Uses regrouping in subtraction	14, 19, 28	30	9, 16

	Intermediate 3	Intermediate 4	Intermediate 5

Numbers and Operations, *continued*

Basic Operations, *continued*

Multiplication

	Intermediate 3	Intermediate 4	Intermediate 5
Models multiplication	54, 55, 57, 60, 61, 62	35	17, 76, 86
Understands the relationship between multiplication and repeated addition	54	27; Investigation 3	13, 17
Multiplies by one-digit whole numbers	56, 59, 61, 64, 70, 76	29, 32, 38	17
Multiplies by two-digit whole numbers	81, 84	44, 48, 87, 90	51
Multiplies by three-digit whole numbers	91, 97	58, 113	55, 56
Uses regrouping in multiplication	84, 91, 97		17, 51, 55, 56
Multiplies by multiples of 10 and 100		67, 85, 86	29, 111
Multiplies by multiples of 1000		85	111
Multiplies decimal numbers		67	109, 110, 111
Multiplies fractions and mixed numbers			76, 86, 120

Division

	Intermediate 3	Intermediate 4	Intermediate 5
Models division	82, 85, 101		87, 96
Divides whole numbers	82, 83, 85, 86, 89, 90, 101	46, 64, 65, 68, 71, 76, 80, 88, 105, 110, 118	19, 20, 22, 26, 42, 54, 92
Understands and uses division notations: division box, division sign, and division bar	82	47, 65	20
Solves division problems with remainders		53, 68, 71, 76, 80, 88, 105, 118	22, 26, 40, 58
Divides decimal numbers		76	117, 118, 119
Divides fractions and mixed numbers			87, 96
Divides by multiples of 10 and 100		105, 110	54

Properties of numbers and operations

	Intermediate 3	Intermediate 4	Intermediate 5
Identifies even and odd numbers	88	10	2
Identifies and uses multiples	78	55	15, 29, 112
Identifies and uses factors		55	15, 18, 25, 80, 82
Understands divisibility		64, 65	25, 42
Uses divisibility rules		64, 65, 105	22, 42
Identifies prime and composite numbers		55	80, 112
Finds the greatest common factor (GCF)			82, 90
Finds the least common multiple (LCM)			112
Uses positive exponents with whole numbers		62	78
Understands the concept of square numbers and square roots	61	Investigation 3	78
Uses the correct order of operations	92	45	24
Learns fact families and understands inverse operations	8, 9, 40, 86, 89	2, 6, 24, 46, 47	8, 10, 14, 19

	Intermediate 3	Intermediate 4	Intermediate 5

Numbers and Operations, *continued*

Fractions, decimals, and percents

	Intermediate 3	Intermediate 4	Intermediate 5
Reads and writes fractions and mixed numbers	5, 29, 41	22, 35, 102	Investigation 2
Locates and names fractions and mixed numbers on a number line	48	37, 102	38
Compares and orders fractions	43, 49	56, 103; Investigation 9	38, 39, 116; Investigations 2, 3
Models a fractional part of a whole	5, 29, 41, 42, 43, 46, 47, 49	26	37; Investigations 2, 3
Names a fractional part of a whole	5, 29, 41, 46, 47, 49	22, 61	30, 60; Investigations 2, 3
Models a fractional part of a group or set	49	70, 95	46
Names a fractional part of a group or set	44, 49	70, 74, 95	30, 46
Finds equivalent fractions	43, 46, 47	103, 109, 115, 116; Investigation 9	23, 79, 81, 90, 91; Investigations 2, 3
Finds the least common denominator (LCD)		116	116
Converts between improper fractions and mixed numbers		89, 104	75, 113
Simplifies fractions		112, 114, 119, 120	81, 82, 90, 91
Reads and writes decimals		4, 22; Investigations 4A, 4B	64, 67, 68, 70, 100, 106
Locates and names decimals on a number line		102	66, 104
Compares and orders decimals		22, 91	69; Investigations 2, 3
Converts between fractions, decimals, and percents		84; Investigations 4A, 4B, 5	30, 67, 71; Investigations 2, 3
Finds a percent of a whole		Investigation 5	30, 43
Finds a percent of a group or set			107
Writes reciprocals of numbers			95, 96
Finds rates and ratios		57, 60	97

Estimation

	Intermediate 3	Intermediate 4	Intermediate 5
Rounds whole numbers	15	20, 42, 54, 117	33, 62
Rounds decimals and mixed numbers		102, 103	101, 104, 106
Rounds money amounts to the nearest dollar	96	20	62
Rounds money amounts to the nearest 25 cents		20	
Estimates sums, differences, and products	30, 92, 93, 94, 95, 99	48, 49, 59, 90, 93	33, 51, 55, 59, 62, 73, 101
Estimates quotients		59, 93	33, 94
Uses compatible numbers	92, 94		

	Intermediate 3	Intermediate 4	Intermediate 5
Algebra			
Patterns, relations, and functions			
Describes and extends an arithmetic or geometric sequence	2, 4, 53, 61	3, 38; Investigation 1	1, 2; Investigation 4
Recognizes patterns in multiplication	54, 55, 59, 61, 64, 76, 78	28	Investigation 4
Completes function tables	25, 34	94; Investigation 11	Investigation 4
Analyzes a pattern or sequence to name a rule		3	1; Investigation 4
Variables, expressions, and equations			
Solves addition equations using concrete and pictorial models	6, 9, 13, 16, 36	1; Investigation 12	11
Solves subtraction equations using concrete and pictorial models	7, 14, 19, 28	25, 31	35
Solves multiplication equations using concrete and pictorial models	55, 57, 61	Investigation 12	
Solves division equations using concrete and pictorial models	82, 85	52, 70	
Writes and solves equations to solve word problems	6, 7, 8, 9, 18, 20, 30, 36, 40, 60, 73	1, 11, 25, 31, 49, 52, 61	10, 11, 16, 21; Investigation 1
Chooses an appropriate formula to solve a problem		62	53, 72, 103, 114
Solves one-step equations with whole numbers	9, 36, 40, 86	31, 49, 52, 68, 70	10, 21, 35
Solves two-step equations with whole numbers		61, 94	49, 62, 72, 84
Geometry			
Basic terms			
Describes and names points	4, 109	23	12
Describes, identifies, and draws segments	Investigation 4	23, 45	31, 32, 61
Describes, identifies, and names angles	65	23, 45	31, 36
Describes, identifies, and draws rays		23	12, 61
Describes, identifies, and draws lines		23, 45	12, 31, 61
Describes planes			32
Properties and relationships of lines			
Describes, identifies, and draws parallel and perpendicular lines	66, 71; Investigation 4	23, 45	31, 32, 45
Describes, identifies, and draws horizontal, vertical, intersecting, and oblique lines		23	12, 31
Angles			
Describes, identifies, and draws acute, obtuse, right, and straight angles	65, 66, 69	23, 63, 78, 81	31, 36, 61; Investigation 10
Identifies and describes interior and exterior angles			Investigation 10
Calculates to find unknown angle measures			Investigation 10
2-Dimensional figures			
Identifies and describes polygons by their attributes	51, 66, 67, 68, 69, 104	21, 63	32, 36, 61
Classifies triangles	69	78	36

	Intermediate 3	Intermediate 4	Intermediate 5
Geometry, *continued*			
2-Dimensional figures, *continued*			
Classifies quadrilaterals	51, 66	63, 92	32, 45
Understands congruence	68	66, 73	32, 36
Understands similarity		66	32
Identifies parts of a circle		21	53
3-Dimensional figures			
Identifies and describes geometric solids by their attributes	71, 75; Investigation 8	98, 99, 100	83
Identifies congruent parts of geometric solids		99	83, 89
Coordinate geometry			
Names and graphs ordered pairs	109, 110; Investigation 11	Investigation 8	Investigation 8
Identifies types of symmetry	Investigations 7, 9	79	88, 105; Investigations 8, 12
Identifies transformations		73, 75, 78, 82	105; Investigation 8
Graphs reflections			88; Investigation 8
Measurement			
Measuring physical attributes			
Uses customary units of length	34, 35, 37, 58	39; Investigation 2	44, 47
Uses customary units of weight	74, 98	77	47, 77
Uses customary units of capacity	87	40	47, 85, 103
Uses metric units of length	79	69, 102; Investigation 2	44, 65, 66
Uses metric units of mass	80, 98	77	77
Uses metric units of capacity	87	40	85, 103
Uses temperature scales: Fahrenheit, Celsius	4	18	27, 98
Measures time	3, 5, 8	5, 54	28
Measures elapsed time		19, 27	28, 35, 108
Chooses an appropriate unit of measurement	34, 74, 79, 80, 87	77	65, 72, 74, 103
Systems of measurement			
Converts in the U.S. Customary System		40, 77; Investigation 2	47, 74, 77, 85
Converts in the metric system		40, 69, 77, 102; Investigations 2, 11	44, 65, 74, 77, 85
Solving measurement problems			
Finds the perimeter of polygons	58, 66, 67	108; Investigation 2	53
Estimates perimeter		111; Investigation 3	101, 104

	Intermediate 3	Intermediate 4	Intermediate 5

Measurement, *continued*

Solving measurement problems, *continued*

	Intermediate 3	Intermediate 4	Intermediate 5
Finds the area of rectangles	53, 62, 63	Investigation 3	72, 115
Finds the area of complex figures		108	103
Estimates area	63	111; Investigation 3	72, 104
Finds the volume of rectangular prisms	72, 73, 77	Investigation 11	103, 104, 114
Estimates volume		111; Investigation 11	104
Finds the measures of a circle			53

Solving problems of similarity

	Intermediate 3	Intermediate 4	Intermediate 5
Solves problems involving scale factor			Investigation 11
Solves problems involving scale drawings: two-dimensional figures			Investigation 11
Solves problems involving scale models: three-dimensional figures			Investigation 11

Use appropriate measurement instruments

	Intermediate 3	Intermediate 4	Intermediate 5
Uses rulers (U.S. Customary and metric)	34, 35, 37, 79; Investigation 4	39, 69, 102	44, 65, 66
Uses a thermometer	4	18	98
Uses a stopwatch		Investigation 4B	69
Uses a compass		21	
Uses a protractor			Investigation 10

Data Analysis and Probability

Data collection and representation

	Intermediate 3	Intermediate 4	Intermediate 5
Collects data	Investigations 3, 6	Investigation 7	Investigations 5, 6, 7, 9
Displays data	105; Investigations 1, 3, 6	83; Investigation 6	Investigations 5, 6, 7, 9
Represents and interprets data using pictographs	Investigations 1, 3	Investigation 6	Investigations 5, 7
Represents and interprets data using bar graphs	Investigations 1, 6	Investigations 6, 10	93; Investigations 5, 7
Represents and interprets data using tables and charts		101; Investigations 6, 8	98, 108; Investigations 5, 6, 7
Represents and interprets data using frequency tables		Investigation 10	Investigations 5, 7, 9
Represents and interprets data using line graphs		Investigations 6, 8	93; Investigations 5, 6, 7
Represents and interprets data using circle graphs		Investigation 6	Investigation 7
Represents and interprets data using line plots		97	Investigations 5, 7
Represents and interprets data using histograms			Investigation 7

	Intermediate 3	Intermediate 4	Intermediate 5
Data Analysis and Probability, *continued*			
Data collection and representation, *continued*			
Represents and interprets data using stem-and-leaf plots			Investigation 7
Represents and interprets data using Venn diagrams			Investigation 7
Chooses an appropriate graph		Investigations 7, 8	Investigations 5, 6
Draws and compares different representations			Investigations 5, 7
Data set characteristics			
Finds the mean, median, mode, and range		96, 97	50, 84; Investigations 5, 7
Probability			
Describes the likelihood that an event will occur	45, 50; Investigation 5	Investigation 10	57
Calculates simple probability		Investigation 10	57, 81
Calculates experimental probability		Investigation 10	57; Investigation 9
Makes predictions based on experiments		Investigation 10	57; Investigation 9
Problem Solving			
Focus Strategies			
Acts it out or makes a model	13, 14, 17	1, 2, 6	12, 52, 120
Draws a picture or diagram	7, 8, 11	9, 10, 12	21, 43, 44
Finds/extends a pattern	1, 2, 3	8, 11, 12	1, 2, 11
Guesses and checks	18, 23, 31	15, 16, 19	18, 22, 26
Makes an organized list	45, 46, 51	24, 36, 46	4, 5, 7
Makes it simpler	67, 68, 69	20, 29, 48	42, 65, 66
Makes or uses a table, chart, or graph	4, 5, 10	3, 4, 5	40, 49, 67
Uses logical reasoning	30, 19, 30	13, 14, 17	3, 6, 13
Works backwards	59, 66, 79	57, 68, 71	13, 14, 16
Writes a number sentence or equation	20, 21, 22	11, 28, 29	17, 28, 32
Communication			
Questions and responds	8, 13, 16	2, 6, 9	2, 3, 7
Works with partners or in groups	1, 2, 6	1, 3, 8	2, 7, 8
Communicates mathematical ideas through objects, words, pictures, numbers, technology, and symbols	3, 6, 8	1, 3, 4	1, 2, 4
Writes about math	51, 56	1, 2, 3	11, 12; Investigation 1
Mathematical Reasoning			
Uses algebraic reasoning	2, 34, 53	3, 94	1, 11; Investigation 4

	Intermediate 3	Intermediate 4	Intermediate 5
Mathematical Reasoning, continued			
Uses spatial reasoning	51, 66, 69, 71, 75; Investigations 7, 9	23, 63, 66, 73, 75, 79, 99	32, 83, 88, 105
Classifies and sorts	67, 69, 102, 104	63, 78, 92, 98	12, 32, 36, 45
Explains an answer	7, 25, 26	4, 5, 6	2, 3, 4
Makes generalizations	2, 4, 12	29; Investigations 1, 2	1, 2, 3
Justifies conclusions	8, 20, 27	11, 13, 15	7, 11; Investigation 1
Connections			
Connects math to geography	21, 31, 33	7, 8; Investigation 1	5, 7, 21
Connects math to history	3, 33, 39	27, 33, 59	5, 30, 33
Connects math to science	3, 4, 5, 18, 20; Investigation 1	9, 11; Investigation 1	4, 24, 27
Connects math to sports	10, 18, 36	19, 32, 36	21, 35, 37

SAXON **MATH**™
Courses 1–3

Scope and Sequence

The Scope and Sequence for the *Saxon Courses 1–3* mathematics series is intended to help educators view the progression of mathematical topics throughout the series. Topics are grouped into nine strands:

1. Numbers and Operations
2. Algebra
3. Geometry
4. Measurement
5. Data Analysis and Probability
6. Problem Solving
7. Communication
8. Mathematical Reasoning
9. Connections

The locators in the Scope and Sequence identify lessons in which direct instruction of a topic is presented. Once a topic is presented, students are continually exposed to the topic in the daily problem sets that follow. Because of space considerations, the daily problem sets are not referenced in the Scope and Sequence. Consequently, student exposure to individual topics is actually stronger than indicated on the following pages.

The locators in this Scope and Sequence indicate where direct instruction on each topic can be found. Locators refer to lesson and investigation numbers.

	Course 1	Course 2	Course 3
Numbers and Operations			
Numeration			
Uses digits	12, 21		
Reads and writes whole numbers and decimals	35, 46	1, 5, 31	12
Understands place value to trillions	12	5	12
Understands place value to hundred trillions		5	12
Uses a number line (integers, fractions)	9, 14, 17, 100	4, 8, 29, 34, 59, 64, 68	1, 10
Uses a number line (rational and irrational numbers)		78, 86	15, 31, 36
Reads and writes numbers in expanded notation	32, 46, 92	4	
Uses comparison symbols (=, <, >)	9	4, 33	1, 77, 94
Uses comparison symbols (=, <, >, ≤, ≥)		4, 78, 93	62, 77, 94
Compares and orders rational numbers	9, 14, 44, 76	33, 86	1, 5, 10
Compares and orders real numbers		100	16
Reads and writes numbers in scientific notation		51, 57, 69, 83, 111	28, 51, 57
Basic operations			
Addition			
Adds integers	3, 5, 10, 100	1, 2	2, 31
Adds decimal numbers	1, 37	1	24
Adds fractions and mixed numbers	24, 26, 59, 61	9	13
Adds algebraic terms			31
Adds polynomials			80
Adds radical expressions			96
Solves addition problems with regrouping	1	2	2, 13, 31
Subtraction			
Subtracts integers	3, 5, 100	1, 2	2, 33
Subtracts decimal numbers	1, 37	1	25
Subtracts fractions and mixed numbers	24, 26, 36	9, 23	13
Subtracts algebraic terms			31
Subtracts polynomials			80
Solves subtraction problems with regrouping	1, 36, 48, 63	23	13, 31, 33
Multiplication			
Multiplies integers	2, 5, 10, 112	1, 2	2, 36
Multiplies decimal numbers	39, 46	1	25, 46
Multiplies fractions and mixed numbers	29, 66, 70	9, 26	22, 23

	Course 1	Course 2	Course 3
Numbers and Operations, continued			
Basic Operations, continued			
Mulitplication, continued			
Multiplies algebraic terms			15, 21, 27, 36
Multiplies radical expressions			96, 120
Multiplies binomials			92
Solves multiplication problems with regrouping	2	2	2
Understands multiplication notations: $a \times b$, $a \cdot b$, $a(b)$	2	1	
Division			
Understands division notations: division box, division sign, and division bar	2	1	
Divides integers	5, 112	1, 2	2, 36
Solves division problems with remainders	2, 11	10, 42, 44	
Divides decimal numbers	45	1	25, 46
Divides fractions and mixed numbers	50, 54, 68	25, 26	22, 23
Divides algebraic terms			27, 36
Properties of numbers and operation			
Identifies even and odd integers	10, 19	4	1
Identifies factors	2, 19, 21	6, 118	9
Identifies multiples	25		
Understands divisibility	21	6	9
Identifies prime and composite numbers	19	21	9
Finds the greatest common factor (GCF)	20	6, 21, 24	9, 10
Finds the least common multiple (LCM)	30	27, 30	13
Uses divisibility tests (2, 3, 5, 9, 10)	21	6	9
Uses divisibility tests (4, 6, 8)		6	9
Finds the prime factorization of whole numbers	65, 73	21, 24, 30, 103, 115	9, 10, 15
Uses positive exponents with whole numbers, decimals, fractions	73, 92	20, 83	15, 27, 46
Uses positive exponents with integers		47, 103	27, 36, 46
Uses negative exponents with whole numbers		57	51, 57
Uses negative exponents with rational numbers			51, 57, 68
Finds square roots	38	20, 100, 103, 106	15, 36, 74
Finds cube roots		106	15
Follows the order of operations	5, 84, 92	2, 52, 63, 85	31, 33
Uses inverse operations	1, 2, 4, 87, 106	2, 9, 106	38
Estimation			
Rounds whole numbers, decimals, mixed numbers	16, 51	29, 33	17, 117
Estimates sums, differences, products, quotients	16	29	17
Estimates squares and square roots	89	29, 100	16, 118
Determines the reasonableness of a solution		29	17
Finds approximate irrational numbers		29, 100	16; Investigation 2

	Course 1	Course 2	Course 3
Algebra			
Ratio and proportional reasoning			
Finds a fractional part of a whole, group, set, or number	6, 22, 77, 117	8, 14, 22, 60, 71, 74	
Writes equivalent fractions	26, 29, 55, 56	15, 24, 27, 48	
Converts between fractions, terminating decimals, and percents	33, 35, 73, 74, 75, 99	8, 43, 48; Investigation 1	11, 12, 71, 119
Converts between fractions, repeating decimals, and percents		43, 48	30, 63, 71, 110
Finds the reciprocals of numbers	30, 50	9, 25	22
Simplifies complex fractions involving one term in numerator/denominator		25, 76	119
Simplifies complex fractions involving two terms in numerator/denominator			119
Finds a percent of a whole, group, set, or number	94, 105, 119	8, 14, 77	11, 48, 58, 63, 109
Works with percents greater than 100%	94	8	67, 71
Solves percent of change problems		92	67, 71
Solves proportions with an unknown in one term	83, 85, 101	39, 81	34, 35, 45, 87
Finds unit rates and ratios in proportional relationships	88	36, 46, 53	7, 29, 34, 38, 44, 49, 105
Applies proportional relationships such as similarity, scaling, and rates	23, 80; Investigation 11	46, 54, 98	26, 49, 70; Investigation 12
Estimates and solves application problems involving percent	105, 119	81, 110	48, 58, 67, 71; Investigation 10
Estimates and solves application problems involving proportional relationships such as similarity and rate		46, 54, 98	7, 35, 45, 49, 64, 70; Investigation 10
Compares and contrasts proportional and non-proportional linear relationships (direct and inverse variation)			34, 41, 47, 69, 98
Patterns, relations, and functions			
Generates an alternate representation of data		56, 116, 120; Investigation 9	69
Uses, describes, and extends arithmetic sequences (with a constant rate of change)	10	4	61, 73
Completes input/output tables	10, 82, 96	16, 56	41, 47, 97, 99
Analyzes a pattern to verbalize a rule	10, 82, 96	4	61, 73
Analyzes a pattern to write an algebraic expression		56, 87	61, 97
Evaluates an algebraic expression to extend a pattern		4, 56	61, 73, 97
Compares and contrasts linear and nonlinear functions		120	41, 88, 98, 99; Investigations 10, 11
Variables, expressions, equations, and inequalities			
Solves equations using concrete and pictorial models	114, 116	87; Investigation 7	
Formulates a problem situation for a given equation with one unknown variable		11, 12, 13, 14	3

	Course 1	Course 2	Course 3
Algebra, *continued*			
Variables, expressions, equations, and inequalities, *continued*			
Formulates an equation with one unknown variable given a problem situation	11, 15, 87, 105	11, 12, 13, 14, 101	3, 4
Formulates an inequality with one unknown variable given a problem situation			62, 77
Solves one-step equations with whole numbers	87	41; Investigation 7	2, 3, 14, 38
Solves two-step equations with whole numbers	106, 116	93, 102, 108, 109	19, 50, 79
Solves one-step equations with fractions and decimals		90; Investigation 7	3, 4, 14, 38
Solves two-step equations with fractions and decimals		93, 108, 110	50, 79
Solves equations with exponents			93
Solves systems of equations with two unknowns by graphing			56, 82, 89
Graphs an inequality on a number line		78, 86	62, 77
Graphs pairs of inequalities on a number line			94
Solves inequalities with one unknown		93	62, 77
Validates an equation solution using mathematical properties		102, 106, 109	19, 90; Investigation 8
Geometry			
Basic terms			
Describes and names points	7	7, 117	18
Describes, identifies, and draws segments	7	7, 117	18
Describes, identifies, and draws rays	7	7, 117	18
Describes, identifies, and draws lines	7	7, 117	18, 44, 54
Describes, identifies, and names angles	28, 69	7, 117	18, 54
Describes planes	28, 69	7, 117	18; Investigation 1
Properties and relationships of lines			
Describes, identifies, and draws parallel, perpendicular, and intersecting lines	28, 71, 97	7, 61, 117	18, 54; Investigation 1
Describes, identifies, and draws horizontal, vertical, and oblique lines	18; Investigation 7	117	44; Investigation 1
Finds and uses the slope of a line		107, 116, 117	44
Properties and relationships of angles			
Describes, identifies, and draws acute, obtuse, and right angles	28; Investigation 3	7, 62	18, 54; Investigation 3
Describes, identifies, and draws straight angles		7	18, 54
Identifies complementary and supplementary angles	69, 71, 97	40	54
Identifies and finds the measures of angles formed by transversals	97	102	54
Constructs an angle bisector	Investigation 8	Investigation 10	
Identifies vertical angles		40	54

	Course 1	Course 2	Course 3
Geometry, *continued*			
Properties and relationships of angles, *continued*			
Identifies adjacent angles		40	54
Calculates to find unknown angle measures	71, 97, 98	101, 102	20, 54, 81, 115; Investigation 3
Properties and relationships of polygons			
Identifies and describes regular polygons	2, 60	18	19
Identifies and describes interior and exterior angles	97, 98	61, 89	
Finds and uses the sum of angle measures	98	40	20, 115
Identifies and draws diagonals		89	66, 74
Understands the effects of scaling on area		Investigation 11	8, 26, 71, 91, 108; Investigation 5
Understands the effects of scaling on volume		98; Investigation 11	35, 71, 76, 91, 106, 108
Understands and applies similarity and congruence	68, 79, 108, 109	18, 97	19
Classifies triangles	93	62	20, 35
Classifies quadrilaterals	60, 64; Investigation 6	75; Investigation 6	Investigation 3
Use Pythagorean theorem to solve problems			
Uses the Pythagorean theorem to solve problems involving whole numbers		99, 112	74; Investigation 2
Uses the Pythagorean theorem to solve problems involving radicals			66, 74, 78, 96; Investigation 2
Uses trigonometric ratios			112, 118
3-Dimensional figures			
Represents three-dimensional figures in two-dimensional world using nets	Investigations 6, 12	67; Investigation 12	55, 95, 100
Draws three-dimensional figures	Investigation 6	67	Investigation 4
Coordinate geometry			
Names and graphs ordered pairs	Investigation 7	56; Investigation 3	41, 89; Investigations 1, 5, 11
Identifies intercepts of a line		116	56, 82
Determines slope from the graph of line		116, 117	44, 56, 113; Investigation 8
Identifies reflections, translations, rotations, and symmetry	108	58, 80	26; Investigation 3
Graphs reflections across the horizontal or vertical axes	108	80	26; Investigation 5
Graphs translations		80	Investigation 5
Graphs rotations			Investigation 5
Graphs dilations			60, 71; Investigation 5
Graphs linear equations		56; Investigation 9	41, 47, 56, 82

	Course 1	Course 2	Course 3
Measurement			
Measuring physical attributes			
Uses customary units of length, area, volume, weight, capacity	7, 31, 78, 82, 102	16, 70, 79, 82	6, 31, 42
Uses metric units of length, area, volume, weight, capacity	7, 8, 82	32, 70, 79, 82, 114	6, 8, 42, 104
Uses temperature scales: Fahrenheit, Celsius	10, 32	16, 32	31
Uses units of time	13, 32	49	80
Systems of measurement			
Converts units of measure in the U.S. Customary System	78, 81, 114	16, 49, 50	6, 52, 72
Converts units of measure in the metric system	7, 114	50, 114	6, 104
Converts between systems	7	50	6
Uses unit multipliers	95, 114	50, 88	52, 64, 72
Solving measurement problems			
Finds the perimeter of polygons, circles, and complex figures	8, 47, 60, 71, 103	19, 65	8, 31, 39, 60
Finds the area of triangles, rectangles, and parallelograms	31, 71, 79	20, 37	8, 20, 37, 60, 66, 92, 96
Finds the area of trapezoids		75	75
Finds the area of circles	86	82	40, 101, 114
Finds the area of semicircles and sectors		104	40
Finds the area of complex figures	107	75	37
Finds the surface area of right prisms and cylinders	Investigation 12	105	43, 44, 85
Finds the surface area of spheres		105	111
Finds the surface area of cones and pyramids			100, 114
Estimates area	86, 118	79	37, 40, 43; Investigation 1
Finds the volume of right prisms, cylinders, pyramids, and cones	120; Investigation 12	95, 113, 117, 119	42, 76, 104, 117
Find the volume of spheres		113, 119	111
Estimates volume	78	117, 119	42, 76, 104, 117
Solving problems of similarity			
Solves problems involving scale factors	83; Investigation 11	98; Investigation 11	26, 35, 87, 91
Solves problems involving similar triangles		97	35, 115; Investigation 12
Solves problems involving indirect measurement		97	65, 118
Solves problems involving scale drawings: two-dimensional	Investigation 11	98	35, 60
Solves problems involving scale drawings: three-dimensional			91

	Course 1	Course 2	Course 3
Measurement, _continued_			
Use appropriate measurement instruments			
Uses rulers (U.S. Customary and metric)	7, 17	8; Investigation 10	
Uses a compass	27; Investigation 8	Investigations 2, 10	39
Uses a protractor	Investigation 3	17, 96	18
Uses a thermometer	10, 100	32	
Data Analysis and Probability			
Data collection and representation			
Collects and displays data	Investigations 1, 4, 5	38; Investigation 5	53; Investigation 6
Makes and interprets tables and charts	Investigation 5	110; Investigation 9	Investigations 8, 11
Makes and interprets frequency tables	Investigations 1, 9	38	Investigation 6
Makes and interprets pictographs	Investigation 5	38	
Makes and interprets line graphs	18	38; Investigation 5	
Makes and interprets histograms	Investigation 1	Investigation 5	53; Investigation 6
Makes and interprets bar graphs	Investigation 4	38; Investigation 5	53; Investigation 6
Makes and interprets circle graphs	40; Investigation 5	38; Investigation 5	Investigation 6
Makes and interprets Venn diagrams		86	90; Investigation 3
Makes and interprets scatterplots			113; Investigation 8
Makes and interprets line plots	Investigations 4, 5	56	53, 109
Makes and interprets stem-and-leaf plots	Investigation 5	Investigation 4	
Makes and interprets box-and-whisker plots		Investigation 4	103
Chooses an appropriate graph	Investigation 5	38	103; Investigations 6, 9
Identifies bias in data collection		38	Investigation 6
Analyzes bias in data collection			Investigations 6, 9
Draws and compares different representations	40; Investigation 5	38; Investigation 5	I 6
Data set characteristics			
Finds mean, median, mode, and range	18; Investigation 5	28; Investigation 4	7, 53, 103, 105
Selects the best measure of central tendency for a given situation		77, 79; Investigation 4	7, 53

	Course 1	Course 2	Course 3

Data Analysis and Probability, continued

Data set characteristics, continued

	Course 1	Course 2	Course 3
Determines trends from data		38	53, 98, 113
Makes predictions from graphs		Investigation 5	98, 113
Recognizes misuses of graphical or numerical information		38; Investigation 5	53
Evaluates predictions and conclusions based on data analysis		38	53

Probability

	Course 1	Course 2	Course 3
Calculates experimental probability	Investigations 9, 10	Investigation 8	32, 59
Makes predictions based on experiments	Investigations 9, 10	Investigation 8	32, 59
Evaluates accuracy of predictions in experiments	Investigation 9	Investigation 8	59
Calculates theoretical probability	Investigation 9	Investigation 8	32, 59, 110
Identifies sample spaces	58	36	32, 68, 83
Calculates simple probability	58, 77; Investigation 9	14	32, 59
Calculates the probability of compound events	Investigation 10	Investigation 8	32, 68
Calculates the probability of the complement of an event	77; Investigation 10	14	32
Calculates the probability of independent events	Investigations 9, 10	94; Investigation 8	32, 83
Calculates the probability of dependent events		94	83
Selects and uses different models to simulate an event			59

Problem Solving

Problem-solving strategies

	Course 1	Course 2	Course 3
Acts it out or make a model	10, 30, 34	34, 50, 54	1, 6, 11
Draws a picture or diagram	1, 14, 17	14, 17, 20	1, 9, 23
Finds a pattern	1, 4, 11	1, 2, 4	5, 10, 16
Guesses and checks	5, 6, 25	5, 18, 19	8, 12, 35
Makes an organized list	2, 26, 32	8, 26, 27	10, 62, 64
Makes it simpler	4, 12, 31	2, 4, 6	4, 7, 13
Makes or uses a table, chart, or graph	11, 14, 59	18, 21, 38	17, 18, 21
Uses logical reasoning	3, 5, 6	3, 5, 7	12, 15, 17
Works backwards	15, 55, 56	6, 15, 35	2, 14, 30
Writes a number sentence or equation	3, 17, 22	3, 7, 9	3, 31, 32

Communication

	Course 1	Course 2	Course 3
Questions and responds	2, 3, 4	2, 4, 6	12, 13, 14
Works with partners or in groups	Investigations 2, 4, 9	Investigations 1, 3, 8	Investigations 1, 4, 9
Communicates mathematical ideas through objects, words, pictures, numbers, technology, and symbols	1, 2; Investigation 2	5, 7, 8	5, 6, 8
Writes about math	4, 6; Investigation 1	11, 12; Investigation 1	3, 4, 5

	Course 1	Course 2	Course 3
Mathematical Reasoning			
Uses algebraic reasoning	10, 11, 82, 87, 96	4, 11, 16, 41, 56, 87	3, 41, 61, 62, 73, 97
Uses spatial reasoning	28, 60, 64, 71, 97, 108, 109; Investigations 6, 12	7, 18, 40, 67, 75, 80, 99, 102, 117; Investigation 11	18, 19, 26, 44, 54, 55, 60, 71, 74, 91, 108, 112; Investigations 2, 3, 4, 5
Classifies and sorts	60, 64, 93; Investigation 6	7, 18, 62, 67; Investigation 6	19, 20; Investigations 3, 4
Explains an answer	1, 2, 3	2, 4, 5	2, 9, 10
Makes generalizations	1, 2, 9	3, 4, 5	2, 3, 7
Justifies conclusions	13, 19; Investigation 1	1, 2, 3	2, 4, 5
Connections			
Connects math to architecture	61, 98	107, 109; Investigation 11	35, 42; Investigation 3
Connects math to art	63, 67, 112	30, 56, 94	31, 33; Investigation 3
Connects math to geography	14, 16; Investigation 1	13, 18, 20	6, 17, 28
Connects math to history	10, 13, 13	12, 13, 14	3, 7, 14
Connects math to science	7, 10, 11	9, 14, 19	16, 18, 28
Connects math to social studies		28, 29, 62	53
Connects math to sports	4, 7, 8	7, 11, 18	3, 4, 6